Beauty for Ashes

The Power of Beauty

Gregory Perry

Beauty for Ashes

Copyright © 2015 by Gregory Perry

Out of the abundance of my heart, I dedicate

the prayers, confessions, and this devotional book to

my dear wife Olawunmi Perry

Table of Contents

THE SKULL AND THE CROSSBONES

To appoint unto them that mourn in Zion, **to give unto them beauty for ashes**, *the oil of joy for mourning, the garment of praise for the spirit of heaviness; that they might be called trees of righteousness, the planting of the LORD, that He might be glorified.*

Isaiah 61:3

"**Beauty for ashes**" is a very powerful phrase. The more I study it, the more I am convinced that nothing is impossible with God. Let us take a closer look at this phrase "*beauty for ashes*".

I was at a hospital one day and I noticed a container sitting off to one side of a room. Two bones behind a skull were printed on this container and I knew that this symbol meant danger. All that I needed to know about the inside of the container was indicated by the symbol displayed on the outside of it. Sometimes symbols are expressed in pictures like the skull and bones and sometimes they are expressed in words. The word phrase "beauty for ashes" contains powerful symbols. In order to understand these symbols and be blessed by them the way God intends us to, we have to take these word symbols apart. Let's start with the word "ashes."

A PLOT TO ANNIHILATE JUDAH AND HER KING

"Ashes" is a word symbol that represents problems, obstacles, deep troubles, disappointments, distress, grief, and mental suffering, but these things are only a few terms that generally describe what the word ashes signifies. When you look up the word ashes in the dictionary you will find that this is one of the definitions– *"the residue that is left after something has completely burned."* So this word ashes really refers to suffering so extreme that there is rarely any left left alive after the suffering has run its course.

In 2 Chronicles 20 there is a historical account of an "ashes" type of event when several armies joined together and became a huge military force to fight against Jehoshaphat and the Israelites. After Jehoshaphat was told about this huge army, fear gripped his heart. Jehoshaphat knew that he and his kingdom were about to me annihilated. In an instant Jehoshaphat's secure domain and his peace of mind turned into ashes. The only way he could escape from this ashes event was through a move of God.

FIGURING OUT WHAT IS REALLY GOING ON

When Jehoshaphat was told that a great multitude was coming against him to reduce him, his people, and his land to ashes, he may have surmised as we can that the Prince of Darkness and his army was behind this plot to annihilate Judah and her king. This military operation was Satan's strategy to destroy Judah completely, but none of Satan's plots to get rid of Judah ever succeeded. This attack against Judah and the well planned out *ashes event* can be partially explained by taking apart the word "annihilate".

Anyone who knows me on a personal level or has watched me teach the word of God, has come to realize that I am a lover of words. There is no way I can preach, teach or even pray without taking apart a word or two or three or more. So let me tell you what I love to do more than anything, except worshiping God, is taking apart words, and putting them back together to determine what is really going on. The word "*annihilate*" comes to us from the root *Nihil* which means – "nothing" or "in vain". This word *annihilate* also has the prefix "*ad*" in front of it. This prefix "*ad*" refers to "moving towards" or "to something". When you unite the prefix "ad" to the root "nihil" it is a picture of a family, a tribe or even a city being wiped off the face of the earth without a trace. So now you know why Satan marshaled this huge military force against Judah; his intention was to wipe all trace of Judah from the earth. That is what he hoped to do.

TAKING A QUANTUM LEAP

Now let us look at the word "beauty." Since the word "ashes" is symbolic for "total annihilation," the the word beauty stands for the way God, through his Holy Spirit, turns the ashes into something that brings glory to His name. God's breakthroughs turn ashes into blessings that create great beauty. When beauty is given for ashes you can experience unrestricted progress. Let me explain what I mean by the unrestricted progress that turns ashes to beauty creates with this short story.

There was a TV show that aired back in the late 80s to the early 90s called Quantum Leap. This was one of my favorite weekly shows. In fact I can remember watching it with my late mother Overseer Louise Perry. The plot of the show revolved around a man named Dr. Beckett. Through an experiment gone bad, Dr. Beckett found himself leaping into bodies of different people from the past. In order for him to get out of the body he was in, he had to first fix what was wrong in that person's life. Although he would fix what was wrong, when it came time for him to leave that body he found himself leaping into another body. One week Dr.

Beckett would leap into a soldier who was fighting on the battlefield. The next week he would leap into a black slave who was running for his life. One time he leaped into a Mafia hit man and then into Elvis Presley! Each leap he took was a sudden, dramatic, and extreme change. As you may imagine, those leaps had a radical impact on Dr. Beckett's emotions.

The phrase quantum leap refers to "a sudden large change." I am not just talking about change but a dramatic change. Not just increase; but a stirring increase. My point is this. When God gives us beauty for ashes it's like taking a quantum leap. His beauty brings significant changes into our lives.

BEAUTY FOR ASHES

In St. John chapter 9 we see an example of what I mean by quantum leap. The chapter opens up with the Lord Jesus taking a stroll down the street. As he's walking he comes across a man born blind. Immediately his disciples asked Him, "*Why was this man born blind? Did he or his parents commit some awful sin*"? Jesus replied by saying, "Neither this man nor his parents sinned." You see his disciples thought that whenever a person went through an unexplained problem, it meant that the person must have sinned. Otherwise they would not be going through this. Jesus stated that "*this man was born blind so that the work of God would be manifested in him*". Jesus told his disciples that sometimes sickness is the result of sin, but, he also made it very clear that there are times when sickness has nothing to do with someone sinning.

Then Jesus did the most amazing thing! He spat on the ground and made clay with his spit. He took the clay, anointed the eyes of the blind man, and said unto him, *"Go to the pool of Siloam and wash."* After the blind man went and washed, he came back seeing. This is what I call a quantum leap or a Beauty for Ashes event. Think about it! Ashes are the result of something that has burned to nothing! Beauty is a result of God taking nothing and turning it into something more than it was to start with.

Now I am going to list 40 prayer points that will give you beauty for ashes. As you pray these prayers, expect God to move powerfully in your life. I also included the Bible verses from which I developed the prayer points. I decree that through these 40 prayers God will breakthrough every stronghold, you will find solutions to all your problems, your helpers will locate you, and no spirit except the Holy Spirit shall have control over your life, in the mighty name of Jesus.

PRAYER POINTS

Prayer Point 1

Deuteronomy 11:26 (KJV)

I choose the blessing, not the curse to operate in my life.

Prayer Point 2

1 Chronicles 4:10 (KJV)
Lord keep me from evil in Jesus' name

Prayer Point 3

Ephesians 3:20 (KJV)
Lord God, let your power work in my life

Prayer Point 4

Isaiah 10:27 (KJV)
By the anointing of the Holy Ghost, it has come to pass;
in my life, that burdens are removed and yokes are de-
stroyed, in the name of Jesus.

Prayer Point 5

Psalm 140:5 (KJV)
Holy Ghost Fire, reveal and destroy every hidden snare set
for my life.

Prayer Point 6

Psalm 68:1 (KJV)
Every enemy of my peace, you must scatter right now, in the name of Jesus.

Prayer Point 7

Isaiah 57:14 (KJV)
Power of God work for me now, remove the stumbling block out of my way.

Prayer Point 8

Genesis 12:2 (KJV)
Spread your right hand over your head and declare this: from today I am blessed to be a blessing, in the mighty name of Jesus

Prayer Point 9

John 5:6-9 (KJV)
By the power of the Holy Ghost, every cycle of failure, is completely broken over my life, in the name of Jesus.

Prayer Point 10

1 John 4:4 (KJV)
According to 1 John 4:4, I declare by the blood of Jesus, I already have the victory over the flesh, the world, and the devil, in Jesus' name

Prayer Point 11

Genesis 50:20 (KJV)
Holy Spirit I thank you that you are using what is meant for evil to bring your goodness into my life, in the mighty name of Jesus.

Prayer Point 12

Luke 10:19 (KJV)
With your help we'll wipe out our enemies, in your name we'll stomp them to dust.

*Prayer Point*s 13, 14, 15

Galatians 3:13-14 (KJV)
Lord, I thank you that the blood of Jesus has redeemed me from the curse of death, poverty and sin, in Jesus' name

Because Jesus hung on the cross, the blessings of Abraham are now available to me, in the name of Jesus.

Holy Spirit purge my life and make me whole, in the name of Jesus.

Prayer Points 16, 17

Isaiah 40:31 (KJV)
According to Isaiah 40:31, I declare that my strength, my courage, and my mind, is being renewed now, in the mighty name of Jesus

The strength I need to walk with God and to fulfill my destiny will never run dry, in the name of Jesus.

Prayer Point 18

Luke 1:37 (KJV)
Lord God, your Word says in Luke 1:37, "There is nothing which you cannot do;" therefore I boldly declare you have given me Beauty for Ashes, in the name of Jesus.

Prayer Point 19

Psalm 7:15 (KJV)
I decree by the power of the Holy Ghost, every pit dug against my life, the one who dug it shall fall into it, in the mighty Name of Jesus.

Prayer Point 20

2 Corinthians 2:14 (KJV)
From this moment on, Beauty for Ashes will keep operating in my life.

Prayer Point 21

1 Corinthians 15:57 (KJV)
By the Grace of God that is resting on my life, I declare victory is mine through our Lord Jesus Christ.

Prayer Point 22

Psalm 5:12 (KJV)
Father, I agree with your word in Psalm 5:12! You surround my life with favor in the name of Jesus.

Prayer Point 23

Psalm 91:7 (KJV)
Lord according to your word in Psalms 91:7--- You are the Protector of my life, in the name of Jesus.

In place of Protector you can also use Defender, Guardian, and Preserver.

Prayer Point 24

Isaiah 65:23 (KJV)
I will not labor in vain but I will finish this year in victory, in Jesus name.

Prayer Point 25

Matthew 15:13 (KJV)
Every plant in my environment and surroundings, that God has not planted, by the fire of the HOLY GHOST be uprooted in the name of Jesus.

Prayer Point 26

Luke 19:41-42 (KJV)
Lord by your Grace and Mercy help me not to miss my opportunity in the name of Jesus.

Prayer Point 27

James 1:22 (KJV)
Every device of self-deception I curse you out of my Life, in the name of Jesus.

Prayer Point 28

2 Corinthian 13:5 (KJV)
Holy Spirit help me to walk the walk not just talk the talk, in the name of Jesus.

Prayer Point 29

Galatians 5:16 (KJV)
As I yield to the Holy Spirit, lust shall not have any control my life, in the mighty name of Jesus!

Prayer Point 30

Psalm 84:12 (KJV)
Lord I trust my total life into your care, in the name of Jesus.

Prayer Point 31

2 Corinthians 2:14 (KJV)
Where ever I am, the Glory of the Lord will manifest, in the name of Jesus.

Prayer Point 32

Matthew 13:43 (KJV)
Holy Spirit by your help I will shine forth as the sun, in the name of Jesus.

Prayer Point 33

John 10:9 (KJV)
Lord Jesus, you are the door to all my breakthroughs, in the name of Jesus.

Prayer Point 34

Isaiah 59:19 (KJV)
Every power that's trying to bleed me dry of my joy, I release a flood of God's Power to flow against you in the mighty name of Jesus.

Gregory Perry

Prayer Point 35

Isaiah 59:19 (KJV)
Lord God I praise you for demonstrating Your power in
my life.

Prayer Point 36

Mark 9:23 (KJV)
Lord I decree that you are bigger and greater than any
mountain in my life, in the name of Jesus.

Prayer Point 37

Proverbs 10:4 (KJV)
Hold out your hands: I prophesy that your hands are
blessed and that you will never beg. By the power invested
in the name of Jesus, I bless your hands now, in the Name
of Jesus.

Prayer Point 38

Lamentations 3:23 (KJV)
Lord God, because of your faithfulness, you will finish you
what you started in my life.

Prayer Point 39

Galatians 3:13-14 (KJV) *There is something I want to remind you of. The blood of Jesus has purchased all of your miracles, breakthroughs, achievements, careers, jobs, and every other good thing. The Lord will add anything missing from your life.*

Everything that is missing in my life that was purchased by the blood of Jesus, I declare them to come into my Life now, in the name of Jesus.

Prayer Point 40

1 John 5:4-5 (KJV)
No spirit except the Holy Spirit shall have control over my life, in the name of Jesus.

Personal Notes

Personal Notes

Personal Notes

Personal Notes

Prophet / Pastor
Gregory Perry

No spirit except
the
Holy Spirit
shall have control over
your life

LIVE! PRAYER CONFERENCE LINE
and Bible Study

Please dial **(712) 432-0075**
then enter **access code 224744** and press #
Mondays from **6pm-7pm**
Bible study from **6pm-7pm**

Lead by

Prophet, Pastor Gregory Perry
GOD'S FAVOR HOUSE OF WORSHIP
&
FRESH OIL INTERNATIONAL MINISTRIES

146 Eliza St Providence, Rhode Island 02909
Pastor Gregory Perry (401) 649-3007

Made in the USA
Middletown, DE
17 January 2020